Time Warriors

Catherine Baker

Editorial consultants:
Cliff Moon and Lorraine Petersen

700031170939

RISING★STARS

nasen
NASEN House, 4/5 Amber Business Village, Amber Close,
Amington, Tamworth, Staffordshire B77 4RP

Rising Stars UK Ltd.
22 Grafton Street, London W1S 4EX
www.risingstars-uk.com

Text, design and layout © Rising Stars UK Ltd.
The right of Catherine Baker to be identified as the author of
this work has been asserted by her in accordance with the
Copyright, Design and Patents Act 1988.

Published 2007

Cover design: Button plc
Illustrator: Aleksandar Sotirovski
Text design and typesetting: Andy Wilson
Publisher: Gill Budgell
Commissioning editor: Catherine Baker
Publishing manager: Lesley Densham
Editor: Clare Robertson
Editorial consultants: Cliff Moon and Lorraine Petersen

All rights reserved. No part of this publication may be reproduced,
stored in a retrieval system, or transmitted in any form by any means,
electronic, mechanical, photocopying, recording or otherwise without
the prior permission of Rising Stars UK Ltd.

British Library Cataloguing in Publication Data.
A CIP record for this book is available from the British Library

ISBN: 978-1-84680-208-9

Printed by Craft Print International Limited, Singapore

WORCESTERSHIRE COUNTY COUNCIL	
093	
Bertrams	02.11.07
J822 BAK	£5.00
WS	

Contents

Characters

Dan Lee   Dan is 14. He often has to look after his younger brother Jason. He thinks Jason is a pain.

Jason Lee   Jason is nine. He just wishes Dan would get off his case.

Sima   Sima lives in the same city as Dan and Jason – but 700 years in the future!

Marok   Marok is a friend of Sima's. Together they hope to find a way to beat Zarkarok.

Zarkarok   An evil ruler who has taken over the city.

The Narrator   The Narrator tells the story.

Scene 1
Late for football

Setting: *a city street.*
There are lots of people about.
Dan and Jason are running
through the crowd.

Dan Jason! Keep up!
If you don't get a move on
you'll be late for football.

Jason You're running too fast!
You always run too fast.
I reckon you're trying to lose me.

Dan I wish! I'd like to lose you –
but I'd get hell from Mum.

Narrator   Dan's in a mood because
he has to take Jason to football.
He often gets stuck with Jason
when Mum's working shifts.

Jason   You're always having a go at me.
You really cramp my style, Dan.

Dan   Okay, I've had it with you now.
You can get to football
on your own.

Narrator   Dan turns round and stomps off.

Jason   Great! I don't need you anyway.

Narrator   Jason runs down the road.
After a minute, Dan turns
round again.

Dan   I guess I'd better go back.
He'll never get to football without me.
Hey – wait up, Jason!

Narrator Jason pretends not to hear Dan.
He keeps on running. Then he stops.
He has seen something lying
in the road.

Jason Awesome! I've got to have that!

Narrator It looks like a football –
but it's a kind of golden colour.
It makes a strange humming noise.
Jason gives it a little kick.

Jason Sweet!

Dan Come on! You're going to be
so late …
Hey – what's that?

Jason It's mine.

Dan Oh yeah? Says who?

Jason Well, I found it.
You're not having it.

Narrator Jason kicks the ball down the road.
Dan runs after it.

Dan Got it! Man – this is one
strange football!

Jason Give it back, you big …

Narrator Both boys grab the ball.
Just then, something amazing
happens.

Dan Am I dreaming, or is this football …
getting bigger?

Jason Yeah – I think so. Wicked!

Dan Get back, Jason!

Narrator The boys step back, but it's too late.
The ball gets bigger and bigger –
and then it snaps open.

Jason Wh-what? That's no football …

Narrator   The ball snaps shut again –
but now the boys are trapped inside!

Dan   You stupid little idiot!
You got us into this!

Jason   Me? It only happened when
you grabbed the football!

Narrator   There is a whooshing noise,
and the ball snaps open again.
Jason sticks his head out of the ball.

Jason   Hey! Look at this!

Dan   It looks like where we were before –
but different.

Jason   Yeah. Look at those tall shiny
buildings!

Narrator   Jason jumps out of the ball.

Dan   Jason! Come back, you twerp!
Oh great – I'd better go with him.

Narrator   As Dan steps out, the ball
shrinks back to football size.
Dan picks it up.

Dan   Jason? Where are you?

Narrator   Jason is going into one of
the shiny buildings.
Dan follows him.

Dan   Jason!

Narrator   Dan sees Jason talking to two people.
They are wearing very strange
clothes.

Jason   Hey, Dan – these are Sima and Marok.

Sima   Greetings.

Marok   Who are you?

Dan   I'm Dan, and this is Jason.
Um … where are we?

Sima   This is the city of Carchester.

Jason   Carchester? No way!
That's where we come from!

Dan   Er – what year is it?

Marok   It's 2709, of course.

Jason   Awesome! That's … oh,
about 700 years in the future!

Sima   You come from the *past*?

Dan   Yeah … I guess so.

Sima   But how?

Marok   Sima – we don't have time for this.
We have to get away from here
before Zarkarok comes.

Jason   Zarkarok? Who's he?

Sima   Zarkarok is evil. He has taken over
the city. Many of us have tried
to stop him, but he is too strong.

Narrator   Suddenly, Marok spots
the golden football.

Marok   Wait – what's that?

Dan   This? Er – I don't really know.
It looks like a football but … it's
weird.

Narrator   Sima and Marok look at each other.
Sima takes out a strange thing
that looks a bit like a book.

Jason   What's this?

Sima   It's a VidBook. Listen.

Narrator   Marok opens the VidBook.
On the screen the boys can see
an evil-looking man.
His voice booms out.

Zarkarok   I am Zarkarok. Hear me.

Jason   He fancies himself, doesn't he?

Dan   Shut up!

Zarkarok   I, Zarkarok, shall rule Carchester
for ever. No one shall stop me.
There is an old story that only
one man can beat me –
the warrior Jandason.

Jason   Catchy name!

Dan   Shut up, I said!

Zarkarok   The story says that one day Jandason
will kill me with a deadly weapon
shaped like a golden ball.

Jason   A golden ball! What – like this one?

Zarkarok But I shall be ready for Jandason.
And anyone who helps me by finding
him, or his golden weapon,
will gain a rich reward.

Sima Your golden ball looks just like
the one in the story.
You are in great danger.

Dan What can we do?

Marok You must come with us. Quickly!
There is no time to lose!

Scene 2
Jason the warrior

Setting: *the city of Carchester, in the year 2709. Dan, Jason, Sima and Marok are running to Sima's house.*

Dan Come on, Jason!
You've got to keep up!

Marok Yes! We must get to Sima's house
before Zarkarok finds us!

Sima Wait – maybe we're going
too fast for Jason.

Narrator They all stop.

Jason No! I'm not a baby.
I can run faster
than any of you lot.

Dan Well, keep up, then!

Jason Hang on, Dan.
I've got a better idea!

Dan Oh yeah?

Sima What's your idea, Jason?

Dan It's bound to be a lame one.

Marok Let the boy speak.

Jason Well – we've got the golden
football, right?

Dan Yup – here it is.

Narrator   Dan throws the golden football
at Jason's head.
Jason catches it.

Jason   Well, maybe it really is the weapon
that will kill Zarkarok.
I think we should try it out.

Marok   You're mad. Zarkarok will destroy you.

Sima   Really, Jason, I don't think that's
a good idea.

Dan   Yeah, shut up, lame-brain.

Jason   You lot are such cowards!
What if this is our one chance
to get Zarkarok?
I reckon I could be that warrior
you were talking about – Jandason!

Dan   You, a warrior? Yeah, right!

Sima   I don't think so, Jason.
In the stories, Jandason is a lot …
well … bigger than you.

Jason   Well, I found the ball.
And my name is
a bit like Jandason.
It *could* be me.

Dan   I can't believe I'm hearing this!

Jason   Anyway, I've got the ball now –
and I'm taking it to Zarkarok!

Narrator   Jason runs off at top speed.
Dan, Sima and Marok look at each
other. Then they run after him.

Dan   That stupid kid! Now I'll have to
get him out of this.

Marok   Don't worry – we'll help you.

Narrator   Jason runs to Zarkarok's command
centre. When Dan, Sima and Marok
get there, Jason is already inside.

Dan   I'll have to go in and get him out.

Sima   I'm sorry – we can't come with you.
             The guards know us and they would
             hand us over to Zarkarok.

Marok   We'll hide out here by the wall.
             If you need help, shout.

Narrator Dan goes into the command centre.
             The guards are busy playing cards.
             They don't try to stop him.
             They think he is just a boy.

Dan   When I find that idiot Jason, I'll …

Narrator The command centre is very big.
             Dan gets lost.
             Then he hears Jason's voice
             coming from a room near him.

Jason   Hey, Zarkarok!
             You've got it coming, mate!

Dan   Oh no!

Narrator   Dan goes into the room.
Jason is holding the golden ball,
and shouting at Zarkarok.
Zarkarok is laughing at Jason.

Zarkarok   You stupid boy! I could kill you –
but maybe it will be more fun
to keep you alive …

Jason   I am the mighty Jandason –
take that, Zarkarok!

Narrator   Jason throws the ball at Zarkarok.
But it just bounces. Zarkarok
heads it.

Jason   Er – can I have my ball back?

Dan   Jason – quick! Let's get out of here!

Zarkarok   Another stupid boy!
Have you come to destroy me too?

Narrator   The ball is bouncing around
the room. Dan catches it.

Dan   I've got to put this where Zarkarok
can't get it.

Narrator   Dan sees an open window.
He chucks the ball out of the window.

Jason   What are you doing?

Dan   Perhaps Sima and Marok will
find the ball and keep it safe for us.
I hope.

Zarkarok   Very well. The fun is over now.
You are prisoners of Zarkarok.
Come with me.

Narrator Zarkarok takes the boys to the prison.
He pushes them into a tiny room.

Zarkarok I should kill you.
But you are just stupid boys.
So instead I will lock you
in my prison – for ever.

Narrator Zarkarok locks the door.
The boys are alone.

Scene 3
Dan the warrior?

Setting: *Zarkarok's prison.*
It is midnight. Dan and Jason are alone.

Narrator	Dan and Jason are asleep in the prison. Suddenly, Jason wakes up.
Jason	Dan! What's that?
Dan	Eh?
Jason	Listen!
Narrator	A noise is coming from the window.

Jason   The window – someone's trying to
              open it!

Narrator   Dan and Jason sit up. Someone is
              taking off the window frame.
              Suddenly Sima wriggles through
              the hole. Sima drops on to the floor
              of the prison.

Sima   Shh! Come with me – now!

Jason   What's going on?

Dan   Shut up! Let's get out!

Narrator   The boys follow Sima
              out of the window.
              Marok is waiting for them.
              He has the golden football.

Marok   Quick! Come with us!
              We must be silent or Zarkarok's
              guards will get us.

Narrator   They run through the silent streets
to Sima's house.

Sima   Come on, you'll be safe here.

Dan   Thanks, Sima. And thanks
for getting us out of Zarkarok's prison.

Sima   Well, we couldn't leave you there!

Marok   When we found the golden ball
outside Zarkarok's command centre,
we knew something must have
happened to you.

Dan   That loser Jason thought
he was Jandason.
Guess what – he wasn't.

Jason   Oi! Butt out, Dan!

Sima   Leave him, Dan.
You both need sleep now.
We'll talk in the morning.

Narrator In the morning, Jason is the first to
wake up.

Jason Where's that golden ball?

Narrator Jason finds the ball by Marok's bed.
Quietly, he picks it up.
He is just walking to the door
when Dan wakes up.

Dan What's going on?
Jason, where are you going?

Jason Er – nowhere. Go back to sleep.

Dan You were going to sneak out,
weren't you? You idiot!

Scene 3   Dan the warrior?

Narrator   Sima and Marok wake up too.

Sima   What's going on, boys?

Dan   This idiot here was sneaking out.

Jason   I wasn't!

Dan   You were!

Marok   Okay, that's enough.
Be quiet, both of you.

Sima   We're all awake now.
Let's have some breakfast.

Narrator   Breakfast is apple bread and
something silver and fizzy to drink.

Dan   This is great – thanks!

Jason   Yeah. I was starving!

Marok   We've got to think what to do next.
You are still in great danger
from Zarkarok and his guards.

Jason   Listen – I still reckon I could be
Jandason. I was just throwing
the ball wrong.
Next time it'll work!

Marok   No!

Sima   I don't think so, Jason.

Dan   Believe me, lame-brain,
there won't be a next time.

Jason   But …

Dan   I reckon I know what to do, though.

Marok   What?

Dan   We have to try again.

Jason   Yeah – that's just what I was saying!

Dan   No, Jason. I reckon one of us
is Jandason – but it's not you!

Jason   How do you work that out?

Dan   Well, we know the golden football
             has strange powers, don't we?
             It got us here, after all.

Sima   Yes, but …

Dan   One of us has to be Jandason.
             Jason's already tried – and it wasn't
             him. That leaves me. I'm going to
             give it a go.

Sima   I really don't think that's a good idea.

Marok   You can't play games with Zarkarok.
             He'll destroy you.

Dan   Or maybe *I'll* destroy *him.*
             It has to be worth a try.

Marok   Listen, you were lucky last time.
             Zarkarok won't let you
             get away with it again.

Dan   Just let me give it a try.

Sima   If Dan really wants to try it,
             I think I know a safer way.

Dan   What's that?

Sima   Well, this morning there will
             be a big crowd of people around
             Zarkarok. We could hide
             in the crowd.

Marok   Yes … then if Dan can't destroy
             Zarkarok, we still have a chance
             of getting away.

Dan   Let's go for it.

Jason   Yeah – then we'll see
             if you are Jandason.
             Bet you're not!

Narrator Dan, Jason, Sima and Marok
              go to Zarkarok's command centre.
              There is a huge crowd of people.
              They hide in the crowd.

Marok   Listen! Here comes Zarkarok!

Zarkarok Greetings, people of Carchester.
              Bow down before me, your ruler.

Narrator   The crowd bow down.
Just in time, Dan and Jason
bow down too.

Jason   Someone has to stop that Zarkarok.
He's such a loser!

Zarkarok   You may stand. Now listen to me ...

Narrator   Zarkarok is about to start a long
speech. Sima whispers to Dan:

Sima   Go on, then. Now's your chance!

Scene 4
Jandason

Setting: *Dan, Jason, Sima and Marok*
are hiding in a crowd.
Zarkarok is giving a speech to the crowd.
Dan is about to try to get
Zarkarok with the golden football.

Zarkarok   This has been a great year
for the city of Carchester.
I, Zarkarok, have …

Dan   Death to Zarkarok!

Narrator   Dan throws the golden football
at Zarkarok. It misses.

Dan   Blast!

Jason   Ha! Looks like you're not
             Jandason either, big bro!

Narrator One of Zarkarok's guards
              tries to catch the football.
              But he drops it.
              The ball rolls into the crowd.

Zarkarok Who dares to threaten
              the mighty Zarkarok?

Sima   Marok! Quick!
             The ball is coming this way!

Marok   Got it!

Zarkarok Death to anyone who threatens
              Zarkarok!

Dan   We'd better get out of here …

Sima   Yes – run! Zarkarok's guards
             are looking the other way!

Narrator   The four friends run for their lives.
Marok throws the golden football
to Dan.

Marok   Come on – this way!
We can hide down this street.

Jason   Too late – I think the guards have
spotted us.

Narrator   The street is a dead end.
Dan, Jason, Sima and Marok are
trapped. Zarkarok and his guards
are coming towards them.

Zarkarok   You! Sima and Marok.
I might have known
you would be behind this.
These stupid boys could
never challenge me alone!

Narrator   The guards grab Sima and Marok.

Zarkarok Now – what shall I do with you?
I know – I'll just kill you. And then
perhaps I'll kill your stupid young
friends. Guards!

Narrator The guards step back.
They pull out their guns
and point them at Sima and Marok.

Dan and Jason No!

Sima Boys – don't try to fight back!

Narrator But Dan and Jason are really, really
angry. They're not going to let
Zarkarok get away with this.

Dan Jason – are you with me?

Jason Yeah!

Narrator Without thinking, they both grab
the golden ball. As they both touch it,
the golden ball begins to get
bigger and bigger.

Marok Sima – look!

Zarkarok What the … ?

Narrator The golden ball is huge now.
It rises into the air.
It moves slowly towards
Zarkarok and his guards.

Zarkarok Guards! Get it away from me!

Narrator But there is nothing the guards can do.

Jason Dan – look! I think we've done it!

Dan Yesss!

Narrator The huge golden ball snaps open.
Then it snaps shut again –
over Zarkarok and his guards.

Zarkarok No! This can't be happening!

Marok Sima! They've really done it!

Narrator There is a flash of golden light
and a loud humming sound.
The golden ball opens.
Zarkarok and his guards are gone –
for ever.

Dan How did we manage that?

Jason Dunno.

Sima I think it worked because you did it
together.

Marok Yes – I get it now!
Jason plus Dan equals Jandason.

Jason So I couldn't defeat Zarkarok
on my own, and neither could Dan.

Dan But together, we did it!

Narrator The golden ball shrinks back
to its usual size. Jason picks it up.

Marok   Sima – there is no time to lose!
We must tell everyone the great news!

Sima   Yes – we have to get the city back
to the way it was before Zarkarok.
Are you coming with us, boys?

Narrator Dan and Jason look at each other.

Dan   No, I don't think so.

Marok   We'll go and spread the news, then.

Sima   Yes. Goodbye – and thank you,
Jandason!

Narrator Dan and Jason are left alone.

Jason   Er – Dan?

Dan   Yeah?

Jason   That was cool.
But I wouldn't mind
going home now.

Dan   Me neither.

Jason   How do we *get* home, though?

Dan   I guess we have to use the golden
               football.

Jason   It has to be worth a try…

Narrator   The boys both put a hand
               on the golden football.
               It starts to grow.

Dan   Here we go again!

Narrator   The ball snaps open and then shuts,
               with the boys inside.

Dan   Wonder where we'll end up this time?

Jason   Home – I hope!

Narrator   There is a whooshing noise,
               and then the ball snaps open again.

Dan   Phew – looks like we're back
             where we started.

Narrator   The boys step out of the ball.
             They are back in their own time.

Dan   Oh well, I guess you've missed football.

Jason   Er – no, I don't think so!
             Look at my watch – there's still
             15 minutes to go till kick-off!

Dan   But we were away for ages!

Jason   Maybe time goes more quickly
             in the future …

Dan   Yeah, maybe. Okay then, let's get
             going, or you'll be late anyway.

Narrator   The ball has shrunk again.
             Jason picks it up.

Jason   Um – I think I'll give football
             a miss today.
             I don't really feel like it any more.

Dan   What? Are you ill?

Jason   No – I just feel like going home.

Dan   Yeah, I know what you mean, mate.
              Come on.

Narrator The boys start to walk home.

Jason   What are we going to do
              with the golden football?
              Do you want to keep it?

Dan   No way! It's far more trouble
              than it's worth.

Jason   I think I'll hang on to it, then.
              You never know, it may
              come in handy one day ...

Dan   No sneaking off to the future
              without me, though!

Jason   Don't worry, big bro –
              I won't be going off
              to the future without you!

Drama ideas

After Scene 1

- As a group, decide what you think will happen next. Will Zarkarok find the boys? What will happen to them?
- Act out your ideas.

After Scene 2

- With a partner, be Dan and Jason.
- What will you say to each other when you are locked in Zarkarok's prison? How will you escape?

After Scene 3

- In your group, act out the end of the scene where Jason, Dan, Sima and Marok are in the crowd and Zarkarok is talking.

- Freeze at the point where Dan is about to throw the football at Zarkarok.

- Then each character can take turns to say what they are thinking at this point.

After Scene 4

- Hotseating: choose two people to be Dan and Jason.

- Everyone else can ask them questions, e.g. what do they think about each other now? How have their feelings changed since the start of the play? Will they ever go back to the future?